Color My Patterns

LOUISE ATHERTON

COLOR MY PATTERNS

2017 Louise Atherton
louiseathertoncoloring.wordpress.com

All rights reserved.

ISBN: 1545107254
ISBN-13: 978-1545107256

COLOR MY PATTERNS

LOUISE ATHERTON

Mindful

COLOR MY PATTERNS

Thoughts

LOUISE ATHERTON

COLOR MY PATTERNS

LOUISE ATHERTON

LOUISE ATHERTON

Kindness

COLOR MY PATTERNS

LOUISE ATHERTON

COLOR MY PATTERNS

COLOR MY PATTERNS

LOUISE ATHERTON

COLOR MY PATTERNS

LOUISE ATHERTON

Deliberation

Friendship

COLOR MY PATTERNS

COLOR MY PATTERNS

COLOR MY PATTERNS

LOUISE ATHERTON

COLOR MY PATTERNS

LOUISE ATHERTON

Indulgence

LOUISE ATHERTON

Observe

Breathe

COLOR MY PATTERNS

LOUISE ATHERTON

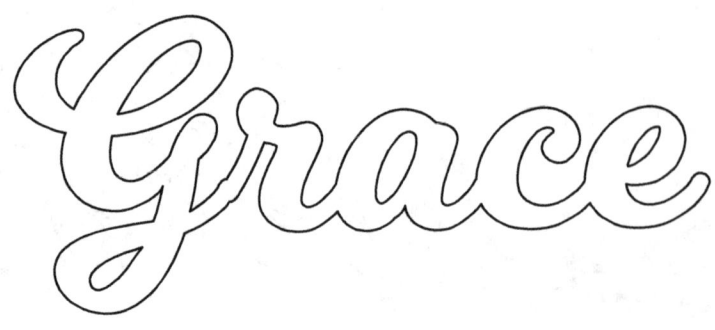

LOUISE ATHERTON

LOUISE ATHERTON

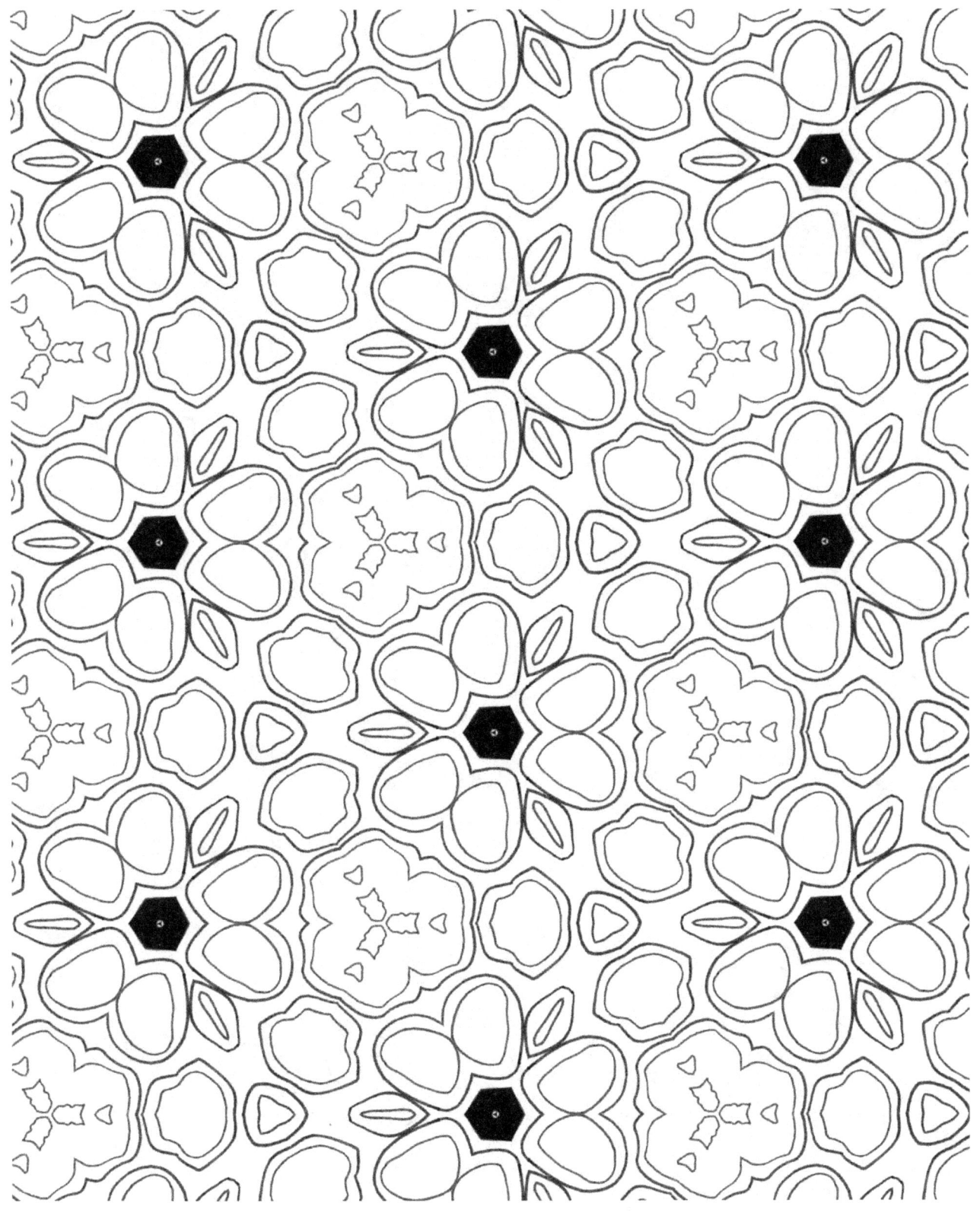

Tolerance

Nostalgia

Planning

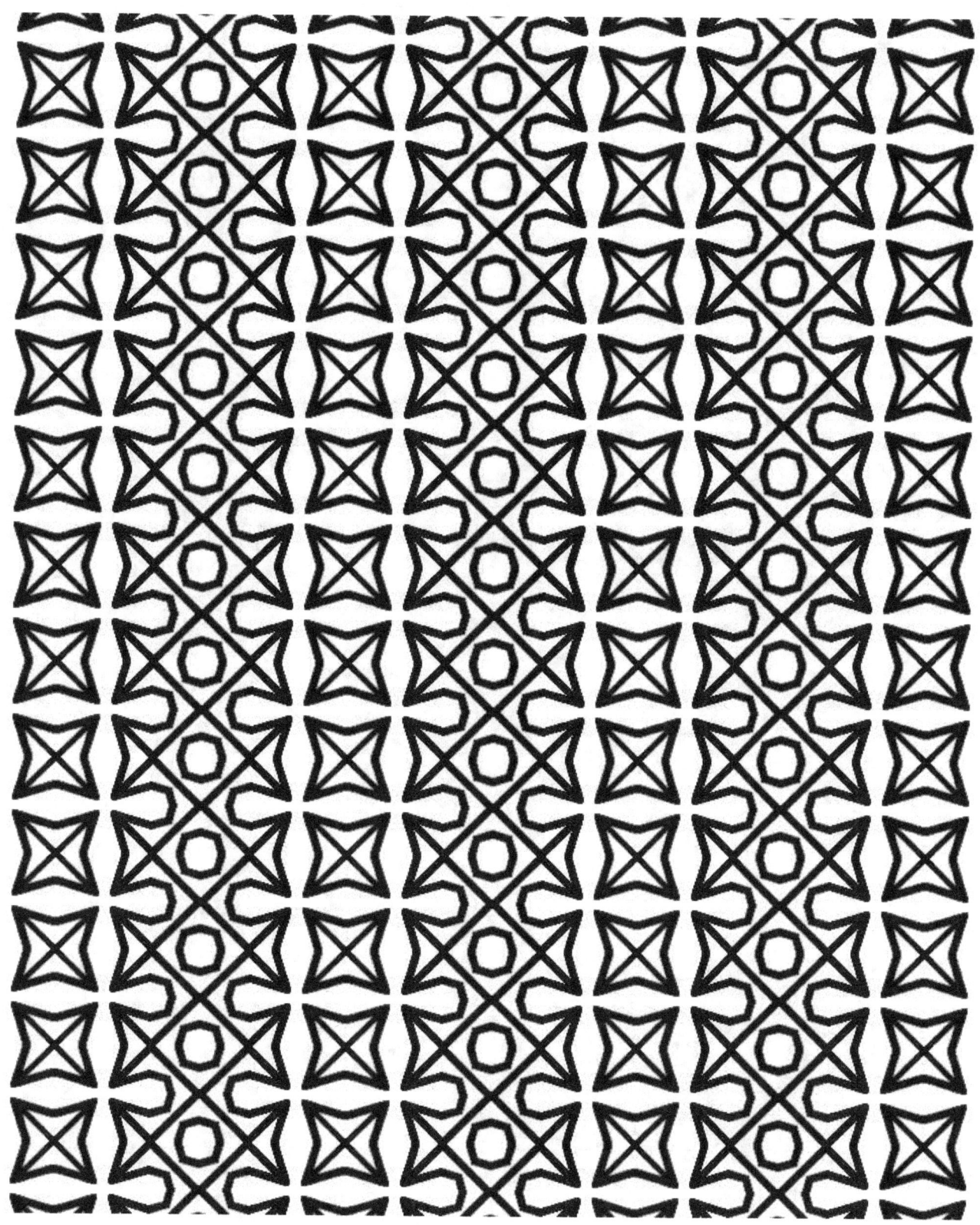

COLOR MY PATTERNS